# Contents

Some words are shown in bold, **like this.** You can find out what they mean by looking in the Glossary.

# Cars

I like cars.

I will tell you my favourite things about cars.

# Different cars

This car is tiny!

This car is so big that my whole class could fit inside it.

# These cars can drive through water!

This car is my favourite.
It is a racing car. It is
very fast.

# Old cars

I like old cars too. I have seen lots of old cars at a car **museum.**

This was one of the
first ever cars.

You had to wind this car
up with a handle!

The first cars were very slow. You could run faster than this old car!

# Taking care of cars

I like helping my dad to take care of his car. We wash it to keep it clean.

We go to the **petrol** station.
Mum fills the car with petrol.

Sometimes, mum puts air in the **tyres**.

Once our car **broke down**. We took it to a garage to be **repaired**.

# Famous cars

I like famous cars. This is the fastest car in the world. It is called the Thrust SSC.

This is Batman's car. It is from a film. I wonder what it is like to ride inside?

This is another famous car. It is called Chitty Chitty Bang Bang.

This car is the star of a film!

# Do you like cars?

Now you know why I like cars! Do you like cars too?

# Glossary

**break down**  when something stops working

**museum**  place where interesting objects are displayed for people to look at

**petrol**  fuel for engines

**repair**  to mend something

**tyres**  rubber ring filled with air that covers a wheel and helps it to grip the road

# Find out more

*Cars: The Essential Guide*, Simon Jowett
(Dorling Kindersley, 2006)

*Getting Around by Car*, Cassie Mayer
(Heinemann Library, 2006)

*Racing Cars*, C. Gifford
(Usborne Publishing, 2004)

# Index

24